AUSTRALIA
MIGRANT
SUCCESS STORIES

NG CHEE MIN

Published in Australia in 2018
by CMN & Associates

Cataloguing in publication data available from the National
Library of Australia

AUSTRALIA – MIGRANTS SUCCESS STORIES
ISBN 978-0-6482582-2-3 (printed paperback)

Author's Note

Australia, as an immigrant nation, has many migrant success stories. Each wave of migration generates its own migrant success stories.

Many of the large corporations in Australia today are the results of the enterprising ingenuity of post-World War II immigrants.

In the professions and in services, there is no shortage of migrant success stories. Many of the migrant contribution goes beyond their adoption countries.

This is the first book in *Emigrate Australia Series*.

Contents

Dr Victor Chang AC – Hong Kong

Fred Hollows – New Zealand

Professor Fiona Wood AM – United Kingdom

Hieu Van Le – Vietnam

Anh Do – Vietnam

Tony Attwood – England

Paula Barlett – Portugal

Jimmy Pham – Vietnam

Many More Success Stories

C - Hong Kong

Er – China

G - China

G – Malaysia

H – Hong Kong

J - China

K – Malaysia

L - Hong Kong

L – Hong Kong

Li – Hong Kong

M - Zimbabwe

N – Malaysia

NH - Pakistan

O - Nigeria

O'Brien – South Africa

O and his wife - Malaysia

Q - China

S – Philippines

S brothers - China

T - Malaysia

T – Hong Kong

W - Burma

A NATION
OF
IMMIGRANTS

Since the arrival of the First Fleet with convicts and free settlers from the British Isles more than 220 years ago, migration to Australia has continued unabated except for the short periods during the 1920s Great Depression years and the two world wars.

Seven million people have migrated to Australia since the 1945's slogan of Populate or Perish by Arthur Calwell Australia's first Minister for Immigration. Three-quarter a million people have come to Australia under the humanitarian stream.

Net overseas migration has become the number one contributor, overtaking natural increase, to Australia's population growth for almost 4 decades since the 1980s.

First The Convicts And Free Settlers

Australia has been a nation of immigrants since British colonisation in 1788. Between 1788 and the late 1860s, over 160,000 convicts were transported to the penal settlements in New South Wales, Van Diemen's land (present day Tasmania), and Western Australia. Other earlier settlers included free settlers seeking a better life and soldiers who stayed on when their term of service was over.

Before federation in 1901, individual colonial administration of the six colonies managed its immigration affairs. The many schemes aiming to attract and assist migrants resulted in more than 700,000 arrivals. The focus was on migration from Europe, with preference for those from the British Isles.

Gold Rush And Population Influx

The discovery of gold outside Bathurst, New South Wales in 1851 and later in Ballarat and Bendigo in Victoria provided the impetus to sizeable arrivals. Some 600,000 people arrived within a decade of the gold discovery. The majority was from Britain and Ireland while other substantial groups included 60,000 from the rest of Europe, 42,000 from China, 10,000 from the United States and 5,000 from New Zealand and the South Pacific.

By 1861, foreign-born accounted for over 60% of the total population in the colonies. Gold discovery in the mid 1890s in Western Australia further boosted the population in that state.

Birth Of A Nation And The 'White Australia' Policy

In 1901, the six colonies in Australia came together to form the Commonwealth of Australia. By then, the new nation had a population of 3.8 million with 23% of the population foreign born and 80% were from the British Isles.

A number of legislations were enacted to formally exclude non-European migrants. The Immigration Restriction Act 1901 marked the start of the 'White Australian Policy' formally excluding non-European migrants with the infamous 'Dictation Test' requiring applicants to pass the written test in any European language. The natives of Asia, Africa and the Pacific Islands (except New Zealand) were excluded from becoming naturalised by the Commonwealth Naturalisation Act 1903.

Almost 400,000 settlers arrived between 1905 and the beginning of World War I. They were mostly from the British Isles. Migration virtually ceased during World War I

Vigorous Migration Programs Post World War I

Australia embarked on a vigorous migration program, including the 'Empire Settlement Scheme' after World War I which resulted in more than 300,000 new settlers arriving between 1919 and 1929. Two-thirds of them were 'assisted' and mostly from Britain.

Migration virtually ceased during the Great Depression years (1929-1937) and thereafter during World War II except for the arrival of 7,000 refugees, mainly Jews of German and Austrian descent from Nazi Germany.

Post World War II Immigration Expansion

Arthur Calwell, the first Minister for Immigration, promoted mass migration with the slogan Populate or Perish. During the period 1945 to 1965, Australia embarked on a post-war reconstruction and immigration expansion program.

Once again, the program was mainly Europe-centric. The programs initiated included:

- Free, assisted passage for British ex-servicemen and their dependents and other selected British migrants, Polish ex-servicemen; schemes for freedom fighters from the USA, Netherlands, Norway, France, Belgium and Denmark; assisted migration scheme with Austria, Belgium, Spain, West Germany, USA, Switzerland, Denmark, Norway, Sweden and Finland.

- 'Bring out a Briton' campaign

- 'Net Egg' scheme for Britons

- The signing of peace treaties with Italy, Romania, Bulgaria and Hungary facilitated migrant arrivals thereafter

- 'Operation Reunion' scheme bringing in settlers from Yugoslavia, Poland, Hungary, USSR, Romania, Czechoslovakia and Bulgaria, to reunite with relatives in Australia

- Resettlement of refugees from Hungary after an uprising there.

The Immigration Restriction Act 1901 was partly relaxed in 1947 allowing non-European business persons who have lived continuously for 15 years to stay without periodic application for permit.

The End Of The 'White Australia Policy'

In 1972, seventy-one years after the enactment of the Immigration Restriction Act 1901, Australia completely dismantled the 'White Australia Policy'. The Whitlam Labour government took further steps in the following year to gradually remove race as a factor in Australia's immigration policies.

In the late 1970s, Malcolm Fraser, the then Prime Minister opened Australia's door to Vietnamese refugees after the first boatload of refugees arrived in Darwin.

The ending of the 'White Australia Policy' has significant impact on Australia's demographic. The Australian population born in Asia has increased many folds.

The ending of the 'White Australia' immigration policy in the 1970s brings another set of success stories – this time from migrants of non-European backgrounds. The Ethnic Business Award entries for the last 30 years have inspiring migrant success stories.

Multicultural Australia

The focus of Australia's migration program has evolved from migrants primarily from the United Kingdom, for the purpose of increasing Australia's population, to a non-racial basis aimed at attracting workers and temporary (skilled) migrants in meeting the skilled labour needs of the economy.

SUCCESS STORIES

The success stories of earlier migrants are in exhibits in museums or documented in research and other publications. A number of museums in Australia are dedicated migration museums - Migration Heritage Centre (Sydney), Immigration Museum (Melbourne) and Migration Museum (Adelaide). Museums in the other capital cities have permanent exhibits and displays on Australian migration history and the migrant success stories.

Sidney Myer – Russia

In 1899, Simcha Baeski joined his brother, who arrived three years earlier, in Melbourne to work with a relative. A few months later, adopting the family name of Myer, the brothers moved to Bendigo to start a drapery shop. Sidney Myer began peddling goods in country Victoria.

In 1911, Sidney Myer bought Wright & Neil, a drapery store in Bourke Street, Melbourne. This marked the beginning of the Myer's retail empire.

Sidney Myer was ahead of his time with employee benefits - offered 73,000 'staff partnership' shares of £1 each on easy terms; shares for executives based on merit, paid vacation, sick fund and even a free hospital within the store.

Sidney Myer's civic leadership and philanthropy during his lifetime were legendary. When he died in 1934, he bequeathed one-tenth of his estate to be held in trust for charitable, philanthropic and education needs. The The Sidney Myer Fund & The Myer Foundation has continued the legacy since.

Vittorio and Giuseppina De Bortoli – Italy

In 1924, Vittorio De Bortolli arrived in Melbourne with "little but his clothes, a few shillings, boundless optimism and a new capacity for hard work". He took a train to Griffith where he worked on farm and winery. Three years later, he bought a 55-acre mixed 'fruit salad' farm in Bilbul near Griffith. His fiancée Giuseppina was working in France saving to join him in Australia. Giuseppina and Vittorio married in 1929. Later the wine-making business expanded and became the main business.

The second and third generations expanded the business further and today De Bortoli is one of Australia's leading wine producers and exporters.

Bing Lee – China

In 1929, Bing Lee came to Australia leaving his family behind and started trading in Chinese handicraft. The family was reunited after the end of World War II. He then bought a fruit shop in Fairfield and ran it with his eldest son.

Bing Lee later bought a small electrical shop - the beginning of present-day Bing Lee retail electrical empire with 42 outlets.

Cees and Johanna Tesselaar – The Netherlands

In 1939 – just weeks before the outbreak of World War II, the couple left Holland on their wedding day aboard the *Strahallan* heading for Australia. They brought little but their farming expertise and a firm belief in hard work and the land of opportunity. In 1945, they planted Tulips and Gladioli in their small newly purchased six-hectare farm in Silvan in the Dandenong Ranges outside Melbourne. They also helped other Dutch immigrants establish their own nursery businesses.

Today, Padua Bulb Nurseries is Australia's largest family-owned floricultural operation. Flowers grown by some 140 growers are also marketed through the Tesselaar network of companies. in Victoria, New South Wales, Queensland and Western Australia.

The annual Tesselaar Tulip Festival, held in October at the Silvan farm, is a major event. Visitors to the farm see blooming tulips and other flowers and members of the Tesselaa family and extended family dressed in traditional Dutch costume and clogs.

Dick Dusseldorp AO - The Netherlands

In 1950, Dick Dusseldorp visited Australia for business opportunities for Bredero's - a large Dutch building company. He secured the joint venture contract for his employer and returned to Sydney a year later with his family and some workers to build 200 prefabricated worker houses for the Snowy Hydro-Electric scheme. The Australian operation was in the name of Civil and Civic. In 1958, he formed Lend Lease with Civil and Civic as the largest shareholder. Later, he created the world's first listed property trust. In the 1960s, Lend Lease acquired Civil and Civic from Bredero's.

When "Duss" (as he was known to his workers) retired in the 1980s, Lend Lease has long been an Australian blue chip and highly regarded for its employee benefits. It introduced staff superannuation entitlement two decades before it became an industry practice in Australia.

Franco Belgiorno-Nettis AC – Italy

In 1951, Franco was sent by his company in Italy to Australia to construct power lines. In 1956, Franco and his colleague Carlo Salteri established Transfiled Pty Limited. In less than 10 years, the company became Australia's most successful company handling projects that ranged from transmission towers to hydro-electricity stations, bridges to oil platforms.

In 1989, the company was awarded a $6b contract to build 10 ANZAC class frigates for the Australia and New Zealand governments. In 1989, the two founders stood down as joint managing directors of Transfield Holdings (as the company was then named) in favour of their eldest sons.

Frank Lowry – Czechoslovakia

Frank Lowry arrived in Sydney in 1952. His work ethic impressed John Saunders, another former refugee who was running a milk bar then. The two later partnered and established a delicatessen in Blacktown. Their business flourished. The partners began to dabble in property and named their property venture Westfield Investments Pty Ltd. In 1958, they sold the delicatessen business to concentrate on the property business.

In 1960, Westfield was listed on the Sydney Exchange. In 1977, Westfield entered the property market in the United States and twenty years later into the New Zealand property market. In 2011, Westfield announced that it has entered the Italy property market by taking a half share in a joint venture to develop a 60-acre site next to Milan's airport.

Today, the Westfield Group has interests in and operates one of the world's largest shopping centre portfolios with 104 shopping centres (housing 23,000 retail outlets and assets under management of $63b) in Australia, New Zealand, the United States, the United Kingdom and Brazil.

Investors who invested in Westfield when it first listed in 1960 and remained as shareholders by the end of the last century would find their initial $1,000 investment worth around $109m (*Westfield Annual Report 2000*).

The 2017 Australian Financial Review Rich List ranked Frank Lowry as the fourth richest person in Australia with estimated net with of A$8.26billion.

Maha Sinnathamby – Malaysia

Maha came to Australia to study civil engineering in 1962. He worked for several organisations before establishing his property business in Perth in 1976. He moved to Queensland in the 1980s and continued his involvement in the property business.

In the early 1990s, Maha secured a large land-parcel in Ipwich with his business partner. Today, Maha's Springfield Land Corporation is developing the 2,860-hectaer land-parcel into Greater Springfield – Australia's first privately-built city and the country's largest planned community.

Maha is ranked 57th in the 2017 Financial Rich List with an estimated wealth of $1.02billion.

Tony and Maureen Wheeler – United Kingdom

The couple arrived in 1972 in Sydney after a 6-month overland trip from Europe with 27 cents between them. In 1973, they started Lonely Planet Publications and published *Across Asia on the Cheap.*

In 2007, the Wheelers sold 75% of their shares in Lonely Planet for £88m. Lonely Planet, by then, has become the world's largest independent guidebook publisher. In 2011, they disposed the remaining shareholding for £42m.

Sam Chong – Malaysia

Chong arrived in 1972 in Sydney from Malaysia for post-graduate engineering study at the University of New South Wales.

After graduating, Chong worked for Rosebery silver, lead and zinc mine in Tasmania. He later worked for several mining companies and settled in Queensland's Bowen Basin. He took on a job with Queensland Coal Mining Management, the forerunner of present day Jellinbah Group where Chong is a founder and shareholder.

In 2011, Chong came on to the "Rich 200" list published by the Business Review Weekly (BRW). In 2017, BRW estimated Chong's fortune at $440m ranks 176 on the list.

Chong has since diversified into property. His Felicity Hotel Group owns several properties in Brisbane including the Four Points by Sheraton hotel. His $325 million Mary Lane Project, with apartments and a five-star Westin Hotel in Brisbane CBD, is due for completion by the end of 2018.

Tetsuya Wakuda – Japan

Tetsuya arrived in Sydney from Japan in 1982 at the age of 22. After working for a year as a kitchen hand, he worked for Sydney chef Tony Bilson. He discovered his love for cooking.

In 1983, Tetsuya partnered with the headwaiter and started *Ultimo*. Six years later, he opened his own restaurant Tetsuya's. The restaurant was popular with daily waiting list. It went on to win many awards and received high ratings. In 2000, Tetsuya's was relocated to Kent Street, Sydney.

Tetsuya's has continued to receive awards and high ratings by international magazines.

In 2005, Tetsuya was conferred with the Medal of the Order of Australia in recognition of his "service to the community and the development of Australian cuisine as a chef, restaurateur and author, to vocational training, and to support for charitable groups."

In 2013, Tetsuya was honoured by the Japanese government as the first ever internationally based chef to be recognised as one of Japan's Master of Cuisine.

In 2016, Waku Ghin, the restaurant that Tetsuya started in 2010 in Singapore, received the Michelin Star in the Singapore's first Michelian Guide. A year later, Waku Ghin, the restaurant located in the marina Bay Sands complex in Singapore received Two Michelin Stars.

David and Vicky Teoh – Malaysia

David and his wife migrated to Australia in 1986. In 1992, David founded Total Peripherals Group (TPG) selling computer hardware, e.g. pcs, printers and services for network. Their customers included federal and state governments. By 2005, the company has become an internet service provider (ISP). In 2008, TPG was listed on the Australian Securities Exchange by a reverse takeover of SP Telemedia.

TPG has grown substantially through organic growth and acquisition since. With its acquisition of Australia's third largest ISP iiNet in 2015, TPG becomes Australia's second-largest ISP by customer volume.

The 2017 Australian Financial Review Rich List ranked the couple 26th richest in Australia with an estimated the wealth of $1.9b.

Ruslan Kogan – Russia

Ruslan arrived in Australia in 1989 with his parents. He grew up in Melbourne, attended Melbourne High School and went on to complete a Business Systems degree at Monash University.

After working for a number of companies, he started Kogan in the parent's garage in 2006. Today, the consumer electronics retail online business turnovers over $300 million annually with customers from around the world.

Ruslan first made it to the BRW Young Rich 200 in 2009 with a reported wealth of $15m. Since then, his wealth has approximately doubled every 12 months. He ranked 4th in the BRW Young Rich 2013.

On 7 July 2016, Kogan.com was listed on the Australian Stock Exchange.

Kerr Neilson – South Africa

Neilson came to Australia in 1983 as the head of retail funds management for Bankers Trust (the present day BT Australia). He started Platinum Asset Management – a boutique international equities firm in 1994.

In 2009, the Neilson Foundation opened the White Rabbit Gallery in Sydney to share with the public one of the world's most significant collections of Chinese contemporary arts. Admission to the gallery is free.

In 2014, the Neilson Foundation and Platinum Assets Management announced their joint funding of 20 scholarships totalling $300,000 annually for five years aimed at encouraging undergraduate students in five Australian universities to major in financial planning. The funding will be reviewed and potentially renewed thereafter.

The 2017 Australian Financial Review Rich List ranked him 40th richest person in Australia with an estimated wealth of $1.44 billion.

The Professions

In the professions and in services, there is no shortage of migrant success stories.

Many of the success stories and the migrant contribution goes beyond their adopted home.

Dr Victor Chang AC – Hong Kong

The late Victor Yam Him Chang came to Australia in 1953 to complete his secondary education in Sydney. In 1962, he graduated with a MBBS from Sydney University. In 1972, he returned from the United States after obtaining a Fellowship in Surgery and joined the cardiothoracic team at St Vincent's Hospital.

Victor Chang is credited with establishing the National Heart Transplant Program at St Vincent's Hospital. The Program has performed more than 1200 successful heart, heart-lung, and single lung transplants at St Vincent's hospital since 1984.

He founded the Australasian-China Medical Education and Scientific Research Foundation sponsoring doctors, nurses and students to work in Australia, enabling them to return to improve the quality of patient care in their own countries. He also sponsored many teams from St. Vincent's to China, Singapore and Indonesia where they shared their medical, surgical, nursing, hospital administration and audio-visual skills and knowledge.

In 1986, he was awarded a Companion of the Order of Australia by the Governor-General. The University of New South Wales conferred Victor the highest degree of M.D. Honoris Causa for "scholarly achievement and humanitarian endeavour".

In 1994, The Victor Chang Cardiac Research Institute, set up in memory of Dr Victor Chang, is dedicated to fighting cardiovascular disease through research.

Fred Hollows – New Zealand

Fred moved to Sydney to become Professor of Ophthalmology at the University of New South Wales in 1965. For the next seven years, Fred chaired the ophthalmology division overseeing the teaching departments at the University of New South Wales as well as the Prince of Wales and Prince Henry hospitals.

The late Fred Hollows has been credited with many achievements both in Australia and overseas. In the late 1970s he headed the National Trachoma and Eye Health Program (NTEHP) in Australia. During the NTEHP, more than 465 communities were visited, about 100,000 people were screened, 27,000 people were treated for trachoma and 1,000 surgeries were performed.

Five months before his death in 1992, Fred together with his wife and supporters established the Fred Hollows Foundation to continue the sight saving work. The Fred Hollows Foundation has now helped restore sight to over one million people in the developing world. Fred received numerous awards. He was named as Australian of the Year in 1990.

Professor Fiona Wood AM – United Kingdom

Fiona Wood and her West Australia-born surgeon husband and their two children arrived in Perth in 1987.

In 1993, Fiona Wood together with scientist Marie Stoner set up a skin culture facility. In 1999, they set up The McComb Foundation with the aim of advancing tissue engineering technology technologies. They moved from growing skin sheets to spraying skin cells; earning a global reputation as pioneers in their field. In 2000, Clinical Cell Culture Pty Ltd C3 was established to distribute the spray on skin technology.

Fiona came to the media spotlight in 2002 when she led the team to work on burn victims of the Bali bombing. The spray on skin technology was used in treating the burn survivors. She has received many awards including Member of the Order of Australia and Australian of the Year for 2005.

Hieu Van Le – Vietnam

In 1977, Hie Van Le fled war-torn Vietnam and arrived with is wife in Darwin in a refugee boat.

Thirty-eight years later, he was sworn in as South Australia's 35th Governor. You can read more of this remarkable journey of His Excellency the present Governor of South Australia,

Anh Do – Vietnam

In 1980, Anh Do was a toddler when his family arrived in Sydney after having experienced two pirate attacks and a short stay in a Malaysian refugee camp.

Since an early age, Anh Do was very determined to help his family financially especially 'to earn money to buy my mum a house'. This dream was realised in Christmas 2000. He was then 23.

He turned down law firm job offers and continued his stand-up comedy interest after graduation. Since then, Anh Do has become a popular actor and comedian including acting in television series and films, a well sought after speaker.

His book The Happiest Refugee – telling his incredible, uplifting and inspiring story – went on to win six book awards in 2011.

Tony Attwood – England

Tony Attwood qualified as a clinical psychologist in England in 1975. He started his practice in Brisbane in 1992.

His book, *Asperger's Syndrome – A Guide for Parents and Professionals*, has been translated into 20 languages and has sold over 300,000 copies.

Tony has many scientific papers and books on the subject. He is also the adjunct professor at Griffith University, Queensland. Tony travels extensively nationally and internationally to present workshops and papers.

Paula Barlett – Portugal

Paula Barrett was born in Angola and lived in Mozambique, Macao and many other places before migrating to Australia from Portugal in 1986 with hardly able to speak any English.

Many told her that she would have difficulty to succeed in Australia without English as a first language. Paula proves the sceptic wrong. She went on to hold adjunct professorship at Australian National, University of Queensland (School of Education) and the RMIT University (School of Psychology).

She was also the founding director of Pathways Health and Research Centre. Its *The FRIENDS for Life* program has long been recognized by the World Health Organization as the best practice for the prevention and treatment of childhood anxiety and depression through the building of emotional resilience.

Jimmy Pham – Vietnam

Jimmy Pham migrated to Sydney as a young child with his mother and siblings. In 1996, aged 24, he returned to Vietnam on a temporary assignment as a tour operator.

He later started KOTO – "Know One Teach One" a social enterprise training disadvantaged kids. For more than a decade, the two centres in Hanoi and Saigon have trained over 400 students with another 200 under training. Many graduates of KOTO work at the KOTO restaurants and other businesses of KOTO or in the hospitality industry.

G - China

G came to Australia from Fuzhou, China to study English in the late 1980s. G was allowed to stay in Australia after the political event in China. After her secondary education in Canton, J came to Australia in 1988 to attend an English course at a private college. J was issued with temporary visa and later a permanent resident visa.

G married a Malaysian-born lawyer and later worked at her husband's law practice. The sole practice flourished as G's language skill has been very useful to service the increasingly large Chinese-speaking clientele. They have two girls. The eldest is studying law at university.

G – Malaysia

G came to Australia to complete his secondary education in the late 1960s.

On completing his university study in the eraly 1970s, he returned to Malaysia and worked initially in his brother's stockbroker firm and later taught accounting at a tertiary institution. He decided to migrate to Australia with his wife.

An astute investor, G retired a couple of years ago with 'impressive nest-egg and large superannuation'. G's wife trained as a pastry chef while in Australia and continues to work in her creative work that she enjoys tremendously.

The have two girls.

J - China

With the help of relatives in the food business, she started a Chinese restaurant. She later married the cook and had two children. J later sponsored his brothers to migrate to Australia.

Her brother, after a short stay at the restaurant, started his own in a nearby suburb. The parents migrated years later under the family migration stream.

J is very happy with the opportunities, the uncomplicated business bureaucracy and the high quality lifestyle available in Australia. She has since sold her successful business after running it for over 20 years.

K – Malaysia

K worked for several years after finishing his secondary school in Malaysia. With the help of the Lee Foundation he managed to secure funding for his trip to England to pursue a nursing course.

On completing his nursing course, K returned to Malaysia and worked for a short time and eventually migrated to Australia.

K worked for several years in hospitals in Melbourne and the Gold Coast before eventually retiring in Melbourne.

K is forever grateful to his school headmaster for securing the funding for his trip to England. His nursing qualification enabled him to migrate to Australia where he has been living and enjoying the many splendid things that the country offers.

M - Zimbabwe

M decided to explore overseas for a more secure future for the family when it became difficult for them to operate the family farm business in Zimbabwe. In 2003, he travelled to Australia meeting up with potential agricultural employers. The family migrated the following year when M took a job offer to manage a potato seed business in South Australia. Two years later the family qualified for permanent residency.

During a holiday trip to regional Victoria to celebrate they bought a house on the way back! The township where the house is located is the last stop before the ski-fields and attracts visitors to the region all year round. M's wife is a chef with international experience. They were enjoying life in their new home and took whatever available work but when a business opportunity came along they were back in business.

N – Malaysia

N graduated with a technical diploma from the Singapore Polytechnic. He left for the U.K. to further his studies after working for a short time in the island state.

On completing his course he and his wife decided to emigrate to Australia as his wife – a trained nurse was able to secure sponsorship and work in Melbourne.

Four decades later, on reflection of their decision to emigrate, the couple is glad of initiating the move to Down Under.

Since his retrenchment a decade ago, N – a Chartered Engineer has been self-employed and 'love the job and retirement is not part of the plan'. His wife has retired and busy enjoying her retirement life.

NH - Pakistan

Pakistan-born NH first knew about the possibility of migrating to Australia while studying for his Masters degree in Environmental Engineering in Bangkok. A few years later while working in Dubai and recently married, he decided to 'move to a country that was safe, prosperous and offered exciting work opportunities.'

In 2000, they migrated to Australia but returned to Dubai after a few weeks when NH failed to get a job. Two years later they returned, this time better prepared. NH got the job he wanted seven months later.

O - Nigeria

O trained as a doctor in Nigeria. He and his wife decided to move abroad to raise their family. They came to Australia under the Skilled migration program.

O is now the paediatric registrar at a public hospital while his wife is the research associate at the school of nursing at the university. They have two children. They plan to become Australian citizens.

O'Brien – South Africa

In 1997, O'Brien decided to move to Australia from South Africa. According to him, escalating crimes and other reasons prompted him to leave South Africa.

He decided on Melbourne for it reminded him of Johannesburg where he came from.

When a senior role was available in the Australian affiliate, he and his family were relocated with the usual relocation benefits.

O'Brien later moved to Sydney to work for a large Australian financial services group overseeing the international division.

O - Malaysia

O and his wife were working at the University Hospital in Kuala Lumpur in 1969. They decided that they wanted to start their family in Australia as the country has a lot to offer.

Years later they realised their dream when health professionals came on the skill migration list. Q continued his specialist practice in Australia. Today, they are proud grandparents. Two of their children are medical specialists and one qualified as a lawyer. Their daughter-in-law and son-in-law are also medical specialists.

Q - China

Like many of his compatriots from China at that time, Q came to Melbourne from Shanghai to study English in the late 1980s. Later, Q and his wife were allowed to stay.

Q started a Chinese newspaper with advertisement income as its main source of revenue. The paper was given away free. With a growing Chinese population, the business prospered. While the newspaper is still being given away free on weekends, the mid-week edition is a paid edition with substantial news and other contents.

Five years after Q started the paper, he and his family moved to a new house on a large allotment. His parents soon joined them in Melbourne.

S – Philippines

S left the Philippines to pursue further studies in Australia. She selected Melbourne for its 'climate, good environment and friendly people.' It is also where some members of her family are.

S has since qualified as a nurse. She and her husband live within walking distance to her work.

S brothers - China

S came to Australia to attend an English language course. S started working part-time at a factory. The following year, his brother aged 21 joined him.

In the late 1980s, the S brothers together with the 37,000 Chinese citizens were issued with temporary visas and allowed to stay in Australia. They were later granted permanent residency.

The S brothers have now lived in Australia for over 20 years. Both are married with children and own successful businesses.

T - Malaysia

After graduating from the university in the early 1970s, T and his wife both found employment in Kuala Lumpur and settled in Petaling Jaya. T later ran a successful business while his wife worked with the government.

In the early 1980s, they migrated to Sydney. T cited his concern for his children's education opportunity and future motivated them to emigrate.

In Australia, they started a small business but sold it 25 years later.They are now grandparents, happily retired after selling the business. All four children are professionals.

V - Vietnam

V and his family decided to flee Vietnam in a fishing boat after the fall of Saigon (present-day Ho Chi Minh City) at the end of the American War in Indo-China.

With three hundred other passengers, they sat tightly together in an overloaded boat packed with supplies for the five-day boat journey to Malaysia. They were fortunate that they did not encounter pirates plying the sea or huge storm.

They eventually landed in the Indonesian island of Riau and stayed in the refugee camp for almost a year before resettling in Australia.

They were welcome by the locals who were mainly Hakka fishermen. V remembers their life in the island was fairly enjoyable as they were able to convert their gold bars to Singaporean currency and buy fish, meat and vegetable from the locals.

After a short stay in a refugee accommodation in Sydney V and his family was provided with a Housing Commission flat in Flemington in Melbourne. It was in 1979 and there were many jobs available. They were able to save and after three years, bought a weatherboard house in Maribynong. Years later, they sold the house and moved to larger two-storey brick house in the same suburb.

V and his wife have since retired and helped to look after their grandchildren. All the three daughters are married and have professions of their own.

W - Burma

The political event in Burma prompted W and his family to migrate to Melbourne in the early 1980s.

After working at a number of jobs, W decided to run a milk bar (corner grocery shop) with his wife assisting him after work and during weekends. W later sold the business and worked for a motor manufacturer till retirement.

Their three children excelled in schools and later graduated with excellent results from universities. The eldest went on to win a scholarship for a post-graduate program. Later, with a group of business colleagues, she started a successful regional medical enterprise and later listed the company.

In their retirement, W and his wife make frequent overseas trips on holiday. They are glad that they made the decision to come to Australia three decades ago.

www.ingramcontent.com/pod-product-compliance
Lightning Source LLC
Chambersburg PA
CBHW020331290526
45785CB00007B/3001